Get It Done

Train Your Brain to Fight Procrastination, Create Optimized To-Do Lists, Enhance Productivity, and Practice Better Habits

By Michelle Moore
michellembooks@gmail.com

Copyright © 2024 by Michelle Moore. All rights reserved.

No part of this publication may be reproduced, stored in a retrieval system, or transmitted in any form or by any means, electronic, mechanical, photocopying, recording, scanning or otherwise, except as permitted under Section 107 or 108 of the 1976 United States Copyright Act, without the prior written permission of the author.

Limit of Liability/ Disclaimer of Warranty: The author makes no representations or warranties with respect to the accuracy or completeness of the contents of this work and specifically disclaims all warranties, including without limitation warranties of fitness for a particular purpose. No warranty may be created or extended by sales or promotional materials. The advice and recipes contained herein may not be suitable for everyone. This work is sold with the understanding that the author is not engaged in rendering medical, legal or other professional advice or services. If professional assistance is required, the services of a competent professional person should be sought. The author shall not be liable for damages arising therefrom. The fact that an individual, organization or website is referred to in this work as a citation and/or potential source of further information does not mean that the author endorses the information the individual, organization to website may provide or recommendations they/it may make. Further, readers should be aware that

Internet websites listed in this work might have changed or disappeared between when this work was written and when it was read.

For general information on the products and services or to obtain technical support, please contact the author.

Table of Contents

Introduction 9

Chapter 1: The Common To-Do List Mistakes You're Probably Making 13

Chapter 2: How to Stop Procrastinating? 37

Chapter 3: Enhance Your Focus 59

Chapter 4: Boost Your Productivity 77

Chapter 5: How to Become More Organized 89

Did you like this book? 97

Reference 99

Endnotes 103

Introduction

Oh, honey, gather around, because I have a tale for you of a younger, sprightlier me, gallivanting through life's buffet with the organizational skills of a squirrel in a nut factory.

Deadlines? Appointments? Promises? I barely knew the meaning of the word. My philosophy was simple: Notebooks are for novices, schedules are for the scared, and a to-do list?

Please, that's practically admitting defeat in the grand chess game of life.

In the rosy glow of my early twenties, floating through life with the ease of a cloud, I could juggle my two whole responsibilities like a pro. But then, bam! Adulthood smacked me in the face like a ton of bricks. Responsibilities multiplied, stakes soared, and my mind couldn't keep up. I was swimming in a pool of obligations, and let's just say, I wasn't exactly Michael Phelps.

There are pearls of wisdom adults try to tell you but in your golden age of youth like, "You need to start acting like an adult. You need to be more responsible." I swatted them away like annoying flies, armed with youthful hubris and misplaced confidence in my punctuality, which, let's face it, wasn't exactly getting a rigorous workout back then.

Turns out, they might have been onto something.

Post college, without pre-made schedules, I felt like a dog walker tangled in leashes, wondering why life thought I could handle twenty metaphorical dogs. The universe, in its infinite sass, chuckled and said "Love, if you can walk one dog, you can walk twenty. It's called adulthood."

The "dogs" were my tasks, and the "walk" was mastering the ancient art of to-do lists. So, you might ask, why am I, the former queen of disarray, preaching the gospel of organization? Because, my friends, I saw the light. I became a to-do list ninja, not through some mystical inheritance or academic rigor, but through sheer will, Google, and an unhealthy dose of YouTube tutorials.

In today's world, knowledge isn't just a luxury—it's a choice. And so is not knowing.

In the digital age, it's really up to you to stay ignorant about... anything, really. And I didn't shy away from what I needed to do: improve my daily management skills.

So, why should you listen to me, a former chaos connoisseur, qualified to preach the gospel of organization? Because I've been there, done that, and got the T-shirt. From disaster to master, I'm here to guide you in getting your ducks—or dogs—lined up.

This book is your fast track to achieving organized bliss. I've gathered all my insights on creating order and discipline in life to help you:

- Nailing every task like a boss;
- Skyrocketing productivity to Henry Cavill-like superman levels;
- Kicking procrastination to the curb;
- Sharpening focus like a laser;
- Organizing your space like Marie Kondo on speed;
- Crafting the perfect, tailor-made to-do list for you.

Ready to transform your life with a to-do list that actually works? Dive into this book and discover all the secrets you've been missing out on. I's not just about getting things done; it's about reclaiming your sanity and finding your calm in the chaos. Let's get listy!

Chapter 1: The Common To-Do List Mistakes You're Probably Making

When I bid farewell to college in my early 20s, keeping up with my everyday tasks and appointments felt like trying to tame a whirlwind. I tried everything I could think to keep myself organized; I went out and bought an agenda, wrote notes on my phone, set calendar reminders on my desktop, and, of course, made countless to-do lists in an effort to ensure I keep everything on track. While getting my work organized felt like a proactive first step, visually mapping out everything I needed to do, my to-do lists and reminders soon morphed into a vortex of frustration and resentment. My to-do list grew quicker than I was able to check items off of it, running on for pages without an end in sight; when I tried to skip around my list to complete easy tasks, I'd find that they were more tedious and time-consuming than I originally anticipated. I was overwhelmed, and I simply didn't have the time or energy in me to put "Have a panic attack" on my to-do list, let alone tick it off.

I know, I'm not alone in my to-do list troubles; people of all ages struggle to effectively manage their time and tasks, because, surprise, it's not something schools bother teaching. Ironically, schools stress the use of an agenda and task prioritization, but put little emphasis on teaching students how to write assignments or create task lists that are effective. More damning, schools often fail to teach students how to manage their time to prevent their work from piling up. Adults, never equipped with these basics, stumble into bad habits trying to wrangle their workload, leading to costly mistakes that sabotage task completion.

Despite the negative experiences many people have when making them, to-do lists can be helpful tools in organizing work and inspiring productivity. Serving as an external memory aid to help you recall everything you need to do; to-do lists help add structure to your day and simplify the chaos of everyday life. Here's the deal: an effective to-do list isn't just a piece of paper or a digital app—it's your secret weapon for mastering time management. It's about nailing those deadlines, prioritizing like a boss, and dodging life's little curveballs that try to derail your day. Because let's face it, who needs that extra stress, guilt, and frustration? A well-crafted to-do list cuts through the chaos, letting you channel your energy into reaching your full potential. And hey, you probably already knew that.

When you sit down to set up your to-do list (if that's your thing) you might wonder how your to-do list could *possibly* be ineffective. Isn't it just a list of work you need to get done? but then chaos kicks in, and you don't accomplish the tasks on your to-do list, and you become bitter, disappointed, stressed, or resigned. To-do lists don't work after all.

While, at face value, to-do lists may seem straightforward, the science behind crafting one can be quite complex. Underestimating the intricacies of an effective to-do list can ultimately render the list ineffective. In fact, studies show that 41 percent of tasks on the average person's to-do list remain unfinished. By studying the pitfalls that people make when creating to-do lists, we can steer clear of crafting unproductive lists in the future.

Mistake #1: The Great Cramming Catastrophe.

The most common mistake people make when writing their to-do lists is cramming too many tasks onto them at once.

Studies show that an individual can juggle up to 150 tasks at a time. While anyone can recognize that this is an unmanageable amount of work, writing all these tasks down can amplify the stress over getting them done.

Mistake #2: The Time Trap.

Another blunder we make with to-do lists is giving ourselves all the time in the world to finish each task. Guilty as charged, right?

Oh, here's a gem we all know but love to avoid: when we have more time, we're less likely to actually meet deadlines because we procrastinate. Most people try to give themselves ample time to complete a task in case they run into any unplanned circumstances, sometimes even failing to set personal deadlines for themselves. While this might seem helpful, it is actually counterintuitive. When you give too much leeway, you create excuses to shirk your responsibilities and take more time than necessary on the task at hand – time that could be better used on other tasks. This kills your productivity; you get less work done, your workflow turns into a hot mess, and important tasks will fall to the wayside, receiving less attention than they should. Also, we dodge completing tasks that have a far-off deadline as a psychological defense against having to do hard work. On the flip side, tasks with stringent deadlines (real or self-imposed) are often completed quicker and with less hesitation because they are perceived as easy, and gives you that sweet satisfaction of crossing it off the list. Adrenaline, perhaps?

Backing up these facts, Parkinson's Law states that "work expands as to fill the time available for its completion," In other words, the more time you give yourself to do something, the longer it'll take to be completed. A very realistic scenario in my mind is that you've got a report due in a week, but it's really a day's job. Yet, there you are, burning the midnight oil right up to the deadline. Setting deadlines actually cuts stress because it sharpens your focus and ups your efficiency. Treat it like a game – challenge yourself with tight deadlines and turn work into a race against the clock Once you complete your challenge, try reducing the amount of time you give yourself the next time you have to do something similar; this internal competition will help motivate you to focus more on your tasks, making you more productive in the long run.

Reflect on your own experiences: ever noticed how cleaning your house can take all day if you let it? It's like magic: the more time you allocate for scrubbing floors and organizing closets, the longer it somehow takes. Set a tight deadline, though, and suddenly you're zooming through tasks like a cleaning tornado. Do you also remember when you had months to complete a project and barely started until the final weeks? Similarly, there must have been a time in your life when you received a project with a crazy-strict deadline and somehow delivered a quality work. That's Parkinson's Law in action.

Why does this happen? When you have too much time, you dive into unnecessary details. Result? The project you hand in could be unfocused, scattered, and filled with irrelevant information that you wasted hours on. By contrast, when you have a strict deadline, you need to be focused on the main problem of the project – you don't have time to contemplate about interesting factoids. Outcome? More concise, to-the-point deliverable, and overall better than the over-researched pamphlet you spent triple the time on, and stressed much more about due to procrastination and perfectionism.

Mistake #3: Screen-time Diversion.

Managing screen time isn't just child's play—it's essential for all ages to maintain productivity and focus. When you're on deadline duty, eliminating distractions is crucial. While it may sound obvious, ignoring the phone, emails, and social media boosts attention and efficiency big time. Stay focused on your tasks and avoid the urge to check notifications or wander into social media rabbit holes. Your mind will thank you for it.

Mistake #4: Treating To-Do Lists as Static.

Our to-do lists often flop because we don't prioritize tasks. While it may feel good to whittle down our lists by crossing off small, meaningless tasks, it is critical that we learn to pick the most important things from our lists to focus on before we move forward each day. Break down those daunting projects into smaller, manageable steps with clear deadlines. This approach not only keeps your brain from frying but also ensures you focus on what truly moves the needle.

To be effective, a to-do list must break tasks into manageable steps that our brains can handle without overload. Each item needs a clear plan and a deadline to keep us on track towards completing what matters most. These mini to-do lists within each task will prevent the brain from becoming overwhelmed and shutting down.

Think of your to-do list as a dynamic tool, always reevaluated and updated to ensure that tasks are appropriately prioritized to meet your needs. While it may seem like life is full of small fires that constantly need to be put out, an effective to-do list can help show you that most of all these fires will blow out on their own without ever requiring your attention.

Lastly but most importantly, your to-do-list needs a clear purpose. If there is no deliberate reason behind it, why would you feel compelled to finish the tasks on it in the first place? Associate your tasks with specific goals. Whether it's paying bills on time to avoid penalty fees or saving money, tying tasks to specific goals fuels motivation and keeps you moving forward."

Exploring Popular Models for Effective To-Do Lists

While we can all benefit from dodging the blunders mentioned earlier, let's be real: no two to-do lists will look the same. There is no one universally effective one-size-fits-all model for writing a to-do list. Rather, your list should fit your personal organizational style to suit your unique quirks and needs."

The "start/end date" to-do list model

Some people find success writing their to-do lists by categorizing tasks with start and end dates—because who doesn't love a good timeline? This approach can help ensure that you are managing your time appropriately by visually laying out the deadlines for each task. By diligently assigning tasks by due date, you get relieved from the stress of missed deadlines or the guilt of procrastination s; your to-do list will outline *exactly* when each tasks needs to be complete, allowing you to focus your time and energy on what is most relevant to your needs each day.

A correct sense of judgment and a reasonable room for flexibility should be added to this model. When you're plotting out your tasks, you've gotta nail down your time game. For example, writing an annual report—it's not a casual two-day affair, especially if you're squeezing in just an hour daily. Make an accurate estimation on how many hours you can realistically chip away at it each day and how much time you need to complete a long project. Like, for real. Don't lie to yourself. Be honest. People tend to give overly generous or nonsensically strict time estimates to their tasks – that's what generates stress. Additionally, assume that your estimate is not completely accurate. Give yourself a 10-percent buffer from the actual completion—think 11 days instead of 10, for instance. Train your mindset to anticipate roadblocks and toss in an extra day for good measure.

If you don't feel confident about your task-length estimation accuracy this to-do list type is not for you, no worries—there are plenty more to-do list models on the horizon.

The "big-spoon/small-spoon" to-do list model.

Others might find success with the start and end date method for their to-do lists, but there's another option that might work better for you: the "big-spoon, small-spoon" method.

Here, your tasks are split into two categories – everything you need to get done (the big spoon), and everything you need to get done on that day (the small spoon). By breaking your to-do list down into two separate lists, you allow yourself to plan out what tasks urgently need your attention in the next 1-2 days, and what tasks can be postponed until a later date. Each task chosen for the daily "small spoon" list should be chosen based on their urgency, difficulty, and deadline.

Personally, I rely heavily on this method. However, my version takes it up a notch to a five-spoon system., I create a simple excel worksheet in my Google Drive account and update it every day based on my daily tasks, or any changed priorities in the future. Visualize this: a five-spoon masterpiece that we'll explore next.

I've even taken the liberty of crafting a sample table below—meticulously breaking down tasks into daily, weekly, bi-weekly, monthly, and seasonal plans. I start from column E, Seasonal, and work backward, setting ambitious seasonal goals and methodically outlining manageable steps in each category. Because who doesn't revel in a well-organized challenge?"

A	B	C	D	E
Today	This Week	Next Week	This Month	Seasonal

The "Big 5" to-do list model.

In this type of to-do list, people are able to prioritize daily tasks by choosing just *five* things they need to complete over the span of 24 hours. It deviates from the big-spoon, small-spoon method in how tasks are selected and structured; while all entries on your Big 5 list must be pertinent and pressing, aim for at least three tasks that can be wrapped up in a cool 30 minutes each, leaving the other two tasks since it is more time-consuming.

Tasks on a Big 5 list can be prioritized by urgency as opposed to difficulty, giving you the freedom to complete them as needed and focus all your energy on what needs to be done at a given time. Focusing on each of these tasks individually can give you a greater sense of accomplishment and let you know that you are working productively on your list each day.

The categorized to-do list model.

Other folks might still prefer a more categorized approach to writing their to-do lists. With a more categorized approach, you are able to focus on tasks related to different areas of your life, allowing you to prioritize tasks based on the facet of your life that needs tending to most.

These lists can range from broad categories (work, family, personal, etc.) or can be broken down by event, allowing several separate to-do lists to run concurrently to help you organize tasks you are trying to finish for specific projects. One upside to categorized to-do lists is that they provide you with a clear picture for achieving your goals. Allowing you to break down larger to-dos into smaller, more manageable steps. Unfortunately, these to-do lists can also be overwhelming for the faint of heart; with multitudes of to-do lists cluttering your desk, there's a risk of biting off more than you can chew in a single day. It's easy to find yourself spread thin, making slow progress as you pick off just one or two items from each list daily.

If you thrive for transparency and love seeing the big picture, this to-do list might be your cup of tea – but you need to be mindful about your time and energy. Even if you have ten categories where you want to accomplish something, don't crowd your daily list with more than five tasks. (Yes, this means that for that day at least five categories will be ignored.) You can juggle with tasks day by day, finding a delicate balance among the categories. There are categories like work and family that will occupy at least one slot of the five tasks on your daily to-do list. Meanwhile, others, like 'yoga goals,' might only demand attention twice a week – unless yoga's your daily mantra, who knows? This model can provide a comprehensive picture about your life's activities, but remember, be realistic about what is achievable each day. You know how the saying goes, we overestimate what we can achieve in a day and underestimate what we can accomplish in a month.

The "Zen" to-do list model.

Another form of to-do list is the most important task list for the Zen junkies. Proposed by Leo Babauta, this method has the user focus on completing each day the three most important tasks (MITs). These three tasks take precedence over all others on their to-do lists until completed. "No matter what else I do today, these are the things I want to be sure of doing,"[1] Babauta emphasizes.

These MITs are linked to specific goals that you may have set for yourself and can be broken down into smaller steps to make them more manageable. By focusing solely on these three MITs each day, you can alleviate the stress of fretting over the rest of your to-do list, ensuring you prioritize what's most essential.

Babauta also advises to do our MITs first thing in the morning; at home or first thing after arriving at work. As the day progresses, distractions multiply, reducing the likelihood of achieving our most crucial tasks.

---

[1] Babauta, Leo. Purpose Your Day: Most Important Task (MIT). Zen Habits. 2019. https://zenhabits.net/purpose-your-day-most-important-task/

The "Kanban" to-do list model.

More advanced to-do listers (or people who are just incredibly busy) might find the Kanban method a game-changer. Using the Kanban method, tech-savvy users can even create digital Kanban boards to manage tasks online seamlessly. – a to-do list, a doing list, and a

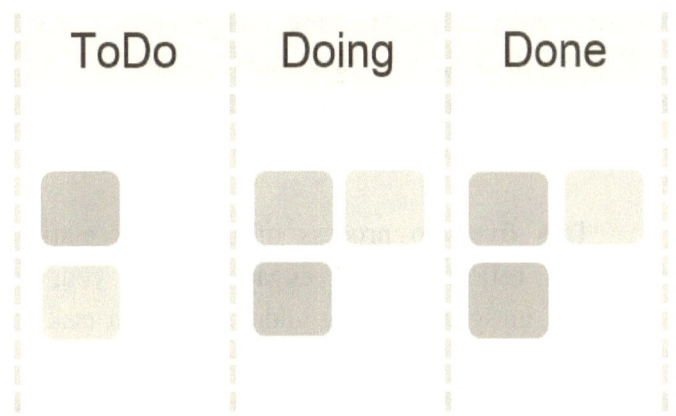

done list – to both physically and visually sort the tasks you are working on.

Picture 1: Standard Kanban Board

The Kanban method allows you to see everything you are working on at one time enabling you to assess your workload effectively and decide if you can handle more tasks., It also fosters a sense of productivity as you shift items from "to-do" to "done" column.

The Kanban method, however, can pose challenges for some users —; with so many tasks moving between columns, it is easy to lose track of the smaller things you need to be doing, causing them to become lost in the shuffle.

The "Getting Things Done" to-do list model

The last form of popular to-do list method we'll explore is aptly called "Getting Things Done," proposed by David Allen as an "easy, step-by-step and highly-efficient method for achieving a relaxed and productive state."

This five-step process of capturing, clarifying, organizing, reflecting, and engaging with your tasks assists you in systematically addressing each task to be able to complete them quickly and effectively. In the capture and clarify phases, you are simply writing down all the things you have to do and determining whether or not they are actionable – that is to say, whether or not you can do anything to address each of these tasks at the given time, thereby reducing the clutter on your to-do list if certain things are not able to be done yet. The organization of tasks in the Getting Things Done method is like staging a grand opera: each task takes on its role, meticulously categorized by the steps needed for its performance. This ensures that when it's time for reflection and engagement, you're not just winging it—you're orchestrating a symphony of productivity.

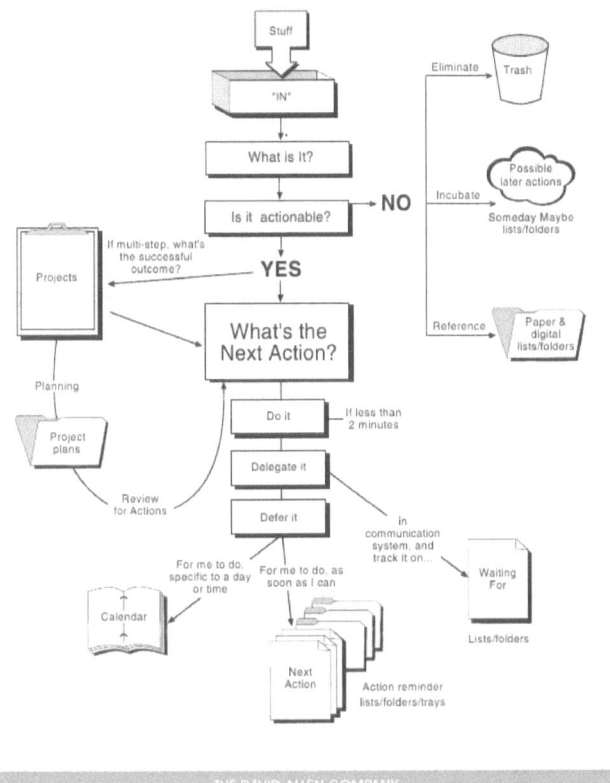

Picture 2: Getting Things Done Model[2]
Your Guide to your Personal to-do-list

---

[2] Allen, David. Getting Things Done. Downloaded in 2019.
www.davidco.com

When you're scribbling down that to-do list, don't just throw things on there willy-nilly. Prioritize like you're choosing between your favorite brunch spots on a Sunday morning. Separate present tasks from future tasks and allocate time for addressing them so that you are able to keep up with all your deadlines This will ensure you're pushing ahead on your to-do list instead of scrambling to catch up on overdue tasks later, thus cutting down on the stress of juggling a million things at once

C'mmon! Take a pen and paper now and write down your:

- most desired long-term goals;
- your recurring tasks; and
- your short-term priorities.

This exercise is crucial for you to identify what really needs to be on your to-do list. Think of it as a reality check. A to-do list isn't just about staying on top of tasks—it's your game plan for daily wins and long-term success. Before you decide which to-do list type you'll adopt, take a good look at "what we are putting up with". So, jot down everything you want for yourself in, say, the next 12 months.

Alright, you've got your grand wish list, your must-dos, and your priorities all scribbled down. Now, let's dive deeper.; Take a moment to figure out why you actually want these goals. When you understand the "why" behind what you are doing, you have a greater sense of urgency behind getting the task done because it is important or even desirable, making the task easier to do. Look, I get it—you're not exactly thrilled about paying your bills. No one is daydreaming about dropping cash on utilities. But you do it to avoid the dreaded late fees. This is a perfectly reasonable "why". Whenever you understand why you are doing something, you are more inclined to want to do it, causing you to procrastinate less.

Now that you're all Zen with your "why," it's time to get strategic about the "how. When you begin to understand why you are doing something, take a moment to look at how you are going to tackle a specific task. Think of it like piecing together a puzzle—one chunk at a time. Break down those intimidatingly big tasks into smaller, bite-sized bits that fit into your schedule. Breaking your tasks down into monthly, weekly, daily, and even hourly increments can make them much less daunting. This approach makes each step feel doable, rather than like climbing Everest in flip-flops. By turning mammoth tasks into manageable actions, you'll find it much easier to actually get things done without feeling overwhelmed.

Got that intimidating list of everything you want to accomplish this year? Yeah, just looking at it might make you want to crawl back into bed. No worries, here comes your savior plan. Grab that paper and flip it over to the blank side. Divide it into 12 columns—nice and symmetrical, like a well-organized spreadsheet.

Step one: Write your monthly recurring tasks into each of the 12 columns, then cross these tasks off from the first page of the paper.

Step two: Estimate how long your short-term priorities will take and slot them into the first three or four columns of the 12-column paper. Imagine you got a thesis to write. Cool, that's about four months of work, assuming you're not chained to your desk 24/7.

Step three: finally, divide and drop your long-term goals into the latter eight columns of your paper. Remember, what seems far off now will soon become a pressing priority.

Now, let's add some deadlines to this masterpiece. Deadlines are like a reality check— you create a reasonable and realistic breakdown of all you need to get done so that you can approach your tasks appropriately. If, for instance, you've got 15 pounds to lose by June for a wedding, starting in May won't cut it.; Rather, you break this goal down to small monthly changes that can be tracked with self-imposed deadlines to give you the best shot at meeting your goal. And here's the kicker: give yourself less time than you think you need. Parkinson's Law is real – "work expands so as to fill the time available for its completion," so, by giving yourself less time, you will feel a greater sense of urgency, which means you're more likely to actually get stuff done and can tweak your plan if things get tricky.

Now, what we've done so far is like the preliminary check-up before the real treatment begins. Think of it as the warm-up before the main event. That yearly plan with monthly rough goals you've created? It's just the starting point.

First, take a hard look at that list and have an honest conversation with yourself. We often get overly ambitious with our future predictions in the present when the burden of hard work is not affecting us. And then when the time comes to put in the work, we flake out– we'll then fail to complete it, setting ourselves up for disappointment and self-doubt. So yeah, I'm giving you a repetitive reminder to be realistic about your plans. Know your limits, understand your "whys", and be honest about what you're willing to sacrifice for your goals.

Once you've weeded out the fantasy from the feasible, it's time to get down to business. Grab another sheet of paper or fire up your to-do list for real.

For those who prefer a more traditional approach, a good excel chart or Google Drive can do the trick. Otherwise, download an online app. Tech-savvies usually use Workflowy, Trello, and Todoist —they're like having a personal assistant in your pocket. Yet again, break your monthly goals into weekly and daily tasks. No matter what type of to-do list you choose to create and maintain, always remember to give yourself time to breathe – stressing over your to-do list is a surefire way to add "Give up on my to-do list" as your top priority.t. Aim for seven to ten tasks per day (depending on the time it will take to complete each task), mixing up quick wins with longer projects, so your list feels achievable and today's tasks don't spill over into tomorrow's to-do list.

As you go about your to-do list, categorize your tasks by nature, type, or location—channel your inner Marie Kondo (similar to the categorized to-do list or the "Getting Things Done" method). When your tasks are broken down by these specifics, you are better able to focus on tasks at the appropriate time. There's no point stressing over an office task that's out of your reach on the weekend. Redirect that energy to tackle the personal life pile-up instead. By pinpointing task specifics, you can cleverly merge errands, reclaiming leisure time like a boss.

While it may seem obvious, one way to avoid a Mount Everest of a to-do list is to ditch unimportant, expired, or undoable tasks from your list – you did this with your yearly goals, now it's time to Marie Kondo your daily ones. Too often, we clutter our lists with tasks that are just not worth our time and energy. Seeing a monster list can make you want to shut down and hide. Again, the best approach is to take the time to cross items off your to-do list that don't matter, the 'unnecessary ones' or are not actively working towards a larger goal – some things are worth simply letting go in pursuit of a greater purpose!

Alright, once your to-do list is clutter-free, it's time to get strategic., Choose your daily tasks and decide how long each one will take to complete. Just a flashback on the above discussion: chunk your tasks as needed. If you've got five items on your list, schedule specific times for each one and mix in some shorter tasks between the longer ones. Setting time frames helps ensure you stick to deadlines and avoid that last-minute panic.

And hey, just because it's your to-do list doesn't mean you can't get some help. If a task needs someone else's assistance, make sure that you communicate this and actively seek the help you need in advance. Everyone has their own priorities, so give them notice to ensure they're available when you need them. By planning ahead, you can dodge the frustration of waiting on others and keep your momentum going strong.

Last but not the least, despite all your meticulous planning and list-making, life happens! Plans go awry and sometimes you'll need to adjust your daily to-do list to accommodate this. Don't fret; roll with the punches and adjust your list as necessary – be flexible when setting deadlines for yourself so that you have some extra cushion built into your schedule. Knowing that your to-do list may change will help you better prepare for these unplanned incidentals and allow you to stay on top of all your tasks.

As crucial as your to-do list is, don't overlook the "done list." Tracking your weekly accomplishments is key. Seeing all you've achieved over time fuels motivation to tackle your to-do list, even when it seems daunting. Eventually, your done list might surpass your to-do list altogether!

Chapter 2: How to Stop Procrastinating?

Ah, procrastination—the eternal struggle we all know too well.

Back in high school, I had this knack for dodging essays like they were a plague. I'd convince myself there were far more important matters at hand—like contemplating the mysteries of the universe or rearranging my sock drawer. So, naturally, when the deadline loomed, there I was at 3 a.m., a cocktail of stress and sleep deprivation, frantically typing away to salvage something barely coherent by 8 a.m. Genius move, huh?

Fast forward to adulthood, my time management skills have definitely leveled up. However, my talent for procrastination still sneaks in. But aren't we all guilty of it? I mean, most of us delayed work for the instant fix of online scrolling, deep dives into social media, or marathon chats with friends. And what happens after that isn't surprising: we find ourselves drowning in the sea of our tasks that have piled up.

To truly grab real happiness and achieve our goals, we must end this procrastination habit and face our responsibilities head-on. By doing so, we can free up more time for guilt-free play (and travels).

But what is procrastination exactly? It's the fine art of delaying something you know you should do. Traditionally, it's a sign of laziness or a lack of motivation. But hold on a sec—sometimes procrastination isn't all bad. Take the gym dilemma, for instance. You finish work smack dab in rush hour, and the last thing you want is to join the treadmill queue with half the city. So, you delay your workout a bit, dodge the traffic chaos, and voila—less frustration, more gains. It's like procrastination has a sensible side, helping you achieve your fitness goals by sidestepping the rush. Of course, like everything else, there's a flip side. Procrastination can also be that annoying monster that messes with our to-do lists.

The thing is, we procrastinate because we're suckers for instant gratification. Someone can show us a task we can check off and revel in that instant rush of accomplishment, and suddenly, we're all in. It's like a little victory dance every time we slash something from our to-do list. We've internalized this craving for quick wins over centuries, favoring the immediate thrill over the distant rewards. This mindset nudges us to push aside those big, time-consuming tasks that don't offer an instant high, throwing a wrench into our plans for those epic, long-term achievements.

Let's be real: humans have a talent for dodging the tasks we'd rather avoid or those that offer rewards in some distant future. So, how do you beat this kind of procrastination? Simple—take action early and get it over with. Sitting around dwelling on how much you dread starting only amplifies the dread, turning reluctance into full-blown frustration.

To burst out of that procrastination bubble, start small. Hate the gym but want to get fit? Start by just putting on those sneakers and stepping outside for a short jog. Once you get going, momentum kicks in, and you're more likely to see it through and cross it off your list. In the next chapter, I'll equip you with some slick techniques so you can finally smash through that mental barrier and dive into action.

Procrastination is not just a nuisance—it can pack a punch that hits your life and productivity square in the gut. Imagine yourself avoiding a crucial chat with your partner because it's awkward. That discomfort brews into toxicity until you're both drowning in it. Or, say you postpone paying that credit card bill—hello, fees that could've been avoided with a quick call? And don't even get me started on ignoring that little belly ache because work seemed more urgent—could spell trouble down the road. Whenever we delay a dreaded task, we're putting our health, wealth, and relationships at risk.

You see, chronic procrastination is like a sneaky little troublemaker that can seriously mess with your life if you let it. So, it's time to get a grip on this before it starts causing chaos. When you finally stop procrastinating, it means that you're finally taking charge. When you stop procrastinating and begin tackling all the tasks you've put off for too long, you take control of your life and reduce your guilt, anxiety, and stress levels. Watch as your professional and personal life thrive, making space for all those awesome experiences that really make life worth living.

Not only does conquering procrastination boost your health, but it's a game-changer for your happiness too. When you finally face those dreaded tasks, it's like a shot of self-respect straight to the soul. Accomplishment? You bet. And that feeling? It fuels your drive to chase after those big, long-term goals. It's a recipe for success, boosting your confidence to be accountable for your own life and smash through those to-do lists like a champ.

Why we just can't help but procrastinate?

As I mentioned earlier, procrastination often gets written off as laziness, but psychological research suggests there's more to it. It turns out, procrastinators aren't just avoiding work—they're getting rid of stress.

Studies reveal that tasks we tend to procrastinate on are usually the tough, boring, or downright unpleasant ones. It's a simple avoidance tactic: why tackle something dreadful now when you can delay the agony?

In her best-selling book 'The Five Second Rule,' Mel Robbins argues that procrastination isn't about attitude, work ethic, or competence. Instead, it's a behavior our brains use to combat stress. We often delay tasks that stress us out, seeking short-term relief through distractions. This behavior has roots in our evolutionary past; our ancestors used stress to avoid real dangers, like saber-toothed tigers. They might have chosen to paint cave walls instead of facing immediate threats. Today, while finishing a Monday paper isn't life or death, our DNA still responds as if it were. Stress equals danger equals 'stay put'—and so we procrastinate.

Next time you catch yourself procrastinating, go easy on yourself—it doesn't define who you are. If you're already in that zone, make the most of it. Take a moment to reflect on these questions to figure out what stressor might be triggering your procrastination:

- Am I stressing over something real, or is it just in my head?

- If what I'm worried about actually happens, what's the worst that could happen to me?

Answering these questions honestly is the first step in developing awareness about why you procrastinate.

I remember planning a solo trip to Japan and kept putting off booking my flights because I was anxious about traveling alone. When I finally asked myself these questions, I realized my fears were mostly in my head. The worst-case scenario was simply a learning experience, and I ended up having an incredible journey, meeting new people, and discovering amazing museums like the team Lab Planets in Tokyo. Sometimes, confronting those uncertainties head-on opens up doors to unforgettable adventures.

While procrastination might have been the go-to stress reliever in caveman days, in today's modern society, it's like adding fuel to the stress fire. Pushing tasks aside just lets them pile up, cluttering our to-do lists with stuff we'd rather avoid. And guess what? Studies back this up: chronic procrastinators deal with more stress, regret, and sleepless nights than those who dive in and get things done. It's a real confidence killer, leaving us stuck in a cycle of guilt and frustration, putting off even more tasks. It's like we're spinning plates, and the pile just keeps growing.

Tips to slay procrastination.

Yep, chronic procrastination is a real tough nut to crack. I mean, the guilt weighs on us, cranks up the stress, and before you know it, we're feeling less capable and just plain down on ourselves. But hey, good news—you can conquer it with these 11 strategies.

1. Take advantage of the "5 Second Rule."

What is the very first thing when you catch yourself procrastinating? **Admit you're stressed**. Don't overthink it—just accept it. Your procrastination isn't about being lazy or incompetent; it's just your brain reacting to stress. Recognizing this helps chill out your mind and lets you think straight instead of diving into self-doubt or avoiding stuff.

Next, make a snap decision that goes against your stress response. It's what Mel Robbins calls her 5 second rule. As she puts it, this is a decision fueled by courage: "When you act with courage, your brain is not involved. Your heart speaks first, and you listen."[3]

Instead of overthinking your stress, flip the script: make a quick decision in five seconds and commit to

---

[3] Robbins, Mel. The Five-Second Rule. Savio Republic. 2017.

working on the very thing stressing you out for the next five minutes. Kick stress by not letting your brain overanalyze. Hate writing that email to your boss? Count to five and start typing! Need to do push-ups? Count it out and get moving! You might only manage twenty push-ups in those five minutes, but that's twenty more than zero. It's not about perfection—just make that 'five-second decision, five-minute commitment' combo and break the stress cycle.

Sure, this practice isn't rocket science, but turning it into a habit? That takes some time. It won't magically cure your procrastination, but it's a solid reminder: you're just five seconds away from making a decision, and what you choose is totally up to you. Kind of comforting, right? Right now, you're just five seconds away from tackling that thing you've been putting off. So why the hell wait?

2. Focus on your "why."

People often procrastinate because they blow tasks way out of proportion, turning molehills into mountains. Treating every little chore like it's the end of the world makes us want to avoid it. When we see every dull task as a looming disaster, we forget why it's important and the sweet rewards waiting at the finish line. Sure, putting off stress might feel good in the moment, but it blinds us to the big wins we could be racking up.

Remember, facing challenges and battling boredom won't kill you, but letting procrastination stress you out might.

Okay, so dieting—ugh, who hasn't groaned at the thought? Watching what you eat can send anyone into a spin. But hey, skipping the diet part won't magically make those jeans fit. Instead of freaking out, zero in on your 'why'. What's driving you? Maybe it's those jeans or just feeling damn good in your skin. It's all about flipping your mindset from dread to determination. Keep that goal in sight and tackle that to-do list like a boss!

If you're lost on your 'why,' no worries—try crafting WHY Statements[4]. Simon Sinek, the guy behind 'Find Your Why,' originally introduced this method to articulate your life purpose.

Here's the template:

To _____ so that _____ .

To stop procrastination, let's focus on the purpose behind the task. Fill the first blank with the task's contribution in your life. What would happen if you finished that dreaded task? The second blank? It's the impact of that action—why it matters so darn much.

---

[4]Sinek, S. (2017). Find your why: A practical guide for discovering purpose for you and your team. Penguin Random House.

For example, let's take Anna, who's getting married in two months and is worried about her bridal dress fitting perfectly. She knows hitting the gym and watching her diet are important, but she's reluctant to start. Then, she suddenly learns about WHY statements and ends up with this:

"To <u>fit the bridal dress</u> so that <u>I can feel and look good on my wedding day.</u>"

Alright, so it sounds basic, right? But for Anna, it means a lot because it's her big day. Just by jotting down her 'why,' she sees why it matters, pushing her to actually do something instead of just sitting around.

Doing your own 'why' thing can totally clear up your goals and get you moving in the right direction.

3. You don't "have to" do anything.

Ever look at your to-do list and see a bunch of 'have tos'? Recently, I realized it's like handing over your power. We all feel better when we call the shots in our lives, right? But when tasks feel forced or imposed on us, bam, hello anxiety central. Remember back when your folks ordered you to clean your room? It was like World War III. But if they threw in a choice—clean your room or wash the dishes—you were more likely to pick one and own it. It's all about feeling like you're in control, not just ticking boxes.

To stop looking at your to-do lists as a "have-to-do" list, change up how you talk to yourself. Seriously, your words matter. Instead of moaning 'I have to,' try 'I choose' or 'I will.'

It's all about tricking your brain into seeing these tasks as something you want to do, not something you're forced into. And here's the best part—add in a 'because' clause. Like, 'I will clean out the closet **because** I'll feel accomplished, satisfied, relieved, proud, happy, free...' You get the picture. It's all about framing it positively, making your brain realize these tasks aren't just chores—they're steps toward feeling awesome.

So, the next time you catch yourself dragging your feet and saying, "I've been putting this off, I just need to suck it up and do it," Try telling yourself, "I can make progress with just one small step. I'm choosing to start now so I can feel accomplished and still enjoy my time later!" Big difference, right? This little language tweak wipes out all those classic procrastinator excuses and shifts the spotlight to the rewards of getting stuff done. By catching those negative thoughts early and turning them into something positive, you're setting the stage for a mindset overhaul. It's all about picking the right words to guide your mindset towards a healthier direction, making way for lasting, positive changes in your life.

Yeah, I get it, it sounds like the classic 'fake it 'til you make it.' But hear me out: every move we make is a choice, even how we talk about it. It's not about pretending to be thrilled about every task—let's be real, some stuff's just dull. It's about knowing there's a payoff. Like tackling that tough job because it's gonna pay off in the end, whether it's a cleaner space or more cash in your wallet. It's all about seeing the silver lining in every pain-in-the-butt chore.

4. Focus on starting instead of finishing.

Most of the stress from to-do lists and tackling those dreaded tasks come from the self-inflicted pressure to just finish, finish, finish. Psychologically, that's a recipe for disaster. When all you see is this perfect, distant finish line, it can mess with your head—cue the anxiety and frustration. Starting a big task and facing that murky path from Point A to who-knows-where? Totally overwhelming. No wonder it brings on stress, frustration, and even a touch of the blues.

Think about a big task like losing weight. Everyone starts with this ideal vision of what they want to look and feel like, right? But real talk, in those early days of hitting the gym and swapping fries for salads, progress can feel slower than a stalled subway train. One slip-up and bam, it's guilt city, anxiety junction, maybe even a side trip to Depressionville. Keeping that perfect-body dream way out in the future? Sure, it works for some, but for most of us, it's about focusing on the here and now. Visualize those early wins—like feeling stronger after a workout or making smarter food choices. It's about evolving that vision over time, embracing your new, healthier self along the way. Stay grounded in the journey, not just the destination—that's the key to staying inspired and reaching your goals.

Instead of overthinking the whens and what-ifs, just focus on that first step. We can debate forever, but taking action right now—that's what kicks things into gear. Starting isn't just the first challenge; it's the rocket fuel to turn dreams into reality. Once you get going, trust me, the rest starts falling into place. Starting is where the magic happens—it's the nudge that breaks the spell of procrastination and gets those tough tasks crossed off your list.

If finding that first step sounds like a chore, try asking yourself, 'What's the smallest, easiest thing I can do right now to move forward?' Just by answering that question, you might find it's as simple as cracking open your laptop or sketching out a quick outline. Once you're in motion, the rest tends to follow. It's all about getting that momentum going!

5. Cut the task into pieces.

Let's talk about big tasks—they're like the Godzilla of stress inducers. Staring down a mountain of work can make anyone want to bury their head in the sand. But I have a simple hack: break it down (if you read it like you're a rapper, it'll sound even better).

Seriously, chop that beast into bite-sized pieces. When you focus on just one chunk at a time, it's like zooming in on the details instead of the big scary picture. Suddenly, it's not so daunting—you're just knocking out one small piece at a time. It's all about tricking your brain into seeing progress, which makes the whole thing less terrifying and actually satisfying.

Think about the last time you sat down to write a report for your boss. Like me, you might have a memory of just looking at that blank screen or piece of paper, unable to write anything. It can feel like scaling Mount Everest in flip-flops, making the whole task seem impossible. However, if you approach it differently—focusing on one paragraph at a time, gradually building up to the larger piece—the task becomes far more manageable.

Breaking down a task like this is key—it gets us rolling on what needs doing, breaks us out of our procrastination cycle, and cranks up our productivity.

6. Ditch those time craters.

Sure, all work and no play might make Jack a dull boy, but at least he's getting stuff done!

Distractions, they're like procrastination's partner-in-crime. To actually finish something, the goal is to laser-focus on the task at hand. Dedicate a chunk of your day to tune out everything so you can zero in on what needs doing.

You probably know it but one of the modern world's biggest distractions is social media. It bombards you with notifications, pulling focus from your work and making it tough to stay productive. Sure, it's tempting to keep those notifications on—FOMO is real—but constantly checking your phone shrinks your attention span and tanks your office game.

In Make Time: How to Focus on What Matters Every Day, Jake Knapp and John Zeratsky coined "time craters"[5] for those pesky distractions that poke huge holes in our days. For instance, you post a quick snap on Instagram,

---

[5] Knapp, J., & Zeratsky, J. (2018). Make time: How to focus on what matters every day. Currency.

thinking it'll take just 90 seconds. But then, half an hour vanishes into thin air because you can't resist checking who liked that post every few minutes.

The ultimate weapon against social media addiction and a productivity boost is to turn off those notifications across all your devices—phone and desktop included. When the pings stop, so does the urge to constantly check for updates. It's a perfect strategy for staying locked in and focused during your workday.

But honestly, just turning off social media notifications isn't always enough to keep distractions at bay. Sometimes, you've gotta lay down the law for yourself—set strict rules on how often you can dive into social media during your workday. These boundaries help you manage your screen time and ensure your breaks aren't all spent scrolling. If sticking to these limits sounds tough, check out a site like www.selfcontrol.com. It locks you out of your favorite time-sucking sites for a few hours, giving you the push you need to knuckle down and get stuff done.

Another trick to tame the social media beast is to practice 'intentional scrolling.' Instead of aimlessly diving into the abyss of endless posts, set a purpose each time you log in. If you're waiting for a reply from your boss, stick to that mission and avoid falling into the bottomless scroll.

7. Gamify your tasks

Since we humans are experts at dodging what we'd rather not do, here's a sweet way to kill that procrastination habit: Make work feel less like a sentence and more like a game.

Basically, gamification is all about making boring tasks more fun by borrowing tricks from games. Think clear rules, goals, feedback, rewards, and challenges that get tougher. It's all about adding that fun factor to tasks that need a boost.

In her book PlayDHD: Permission to Play… A Prescription for Adults with ADHD, Kirsten Milliken, PhD, PCC introduces a clever way to gamify your path to productivity.

It's actually pretty simple (and fun!): first, jot down your 'sucky tasks'[6] and the rewards that light you up, then assign them some points. You can adjust these scores as you go, but the trick is to stay on track and keep your eyes on the prize you're aiming for.

Sucky Tasks	Reward
Organizing receipts, 5 points	Fine dining experience, 10 points
Sorting through emails, 15 points	Buy new journal, 20 points
House general cleaning, 20 points	Date with boyfriend, 30 points

Imagine you're itching to snag that new journal. To earn it, you've got to rack up 20 points first. That could involve sorting through your receipts (3 points) and tackling your overflowing inbox (15 points).

Once you've set your sights on those rewards and started tallying up those points, you'll find yourself more motivated and focused than ever to tackle those dreaded tasks head-on and beat procrastination.

8. Drop perfectionism.

Many procrastinators are hardcore perfectionists. They're all about nailing every task perfectly, so they're like, "Nah, not starting until I've got all the time, resources, and mojo to do it flawlessly." But guess what? This all-or-nothing mentality isn't helpful at all. It's a total productivity buzzkill. Nothing ever really gets off the ground with that approach.

In the mind of a perfectionist, anything less than perfect equals failure. It's like this super damaging mindset, especially if you're trying to crank up your productivity. Sure, being a perfectionist might seem like a badge of honor at work, but in reality, it's a stress factory. Instead of celebrating just getting the work done, you're sweating over every tiny detail being flawless. Remember back in school? Shooting for that perfect 100% on tests was the goal, but getting an 80% or 90%? Didn't exactly derail your life, did it? Same deal in the grown-up world—your work doesn't have to be perfect to be damn good.

Perfectionists, bless their stressed-out souls, often deal with anxiety more than most, which pushes them into some not-so-healthy coping mechanisms. See, perfectionism becomes this handy excuse for procrastination. They'll swear up and down that they can't possibly do a task perfectly with the time, resources, or headspace they've got, so they'll just... uh, put it off indefinitely. And that, my friend, starts this nasty cycle of guilt and stress that's a real self-esteem crusher.

Ditching perfectionism isn't a walk in the park. It starts with admitting that chasing perfection is like trying to catch fog—it's impossible and sets you up for a never-ending cycle of disappointment and self-critique. Instead of obsessing over flawless outcomes, think about what you can actually control: finishing the job. When you prioritize completion over perfection, suddenly your to-do list becomes a conquerable mountain rather than an unscalable peak.

If you're struggling to let go of those perfectionist tendencies, do a quick reality check. Ask yourself, **"Is the endless pursuit of perfection really worth it in terms of time and effort compared to just getting it done?"**

It's a question you gotta ask yourself whenever that urge to perfect something makes you stall. Odds are, there's a whole bunch of better ways to spend your time! Take that energy you'd sink into perfecting one thing and knock out another task on your list. Or better, treat yourself to a self-date with a killer podcast or that audiobook you've been dying to dive into.

Still not sold on ditching perfectionism? Try thinking differently about mistakes—they're opportunities for learning. I mean, every slip-up is literally a chance to grow, personally and professionally. Remember that report blunder you stressed over? Sure, it wasn't ideal, but did all that worry really pay off? Nah. If it eases your mind, think about the worst-case scenario for making an error—chances are, a hiccup won't cost you your job.

Break free from the perfectionist trap by aiming to be better than yesterday. Pursue excellence in everything you do, even when you feel unprepared. When your focus shifts to achieving excellence, every step you take towards your goal becomes progress towards perfection, enabling you to accomplish tasks even when you're not fully ready.

9. Forgive yourself.

People who often procrastinate may carry guilt about their past inaction, leading to lower self-esteem and motivation for future tasks. Whether you're a chronic procrastinator or have recently fallen behind on responsibilities, it's never too late to shake off negative self-talk. Evolution, baby! Tell that nagging voice in your head that insists you "should have" started sooner, or calls you lazy and worthless, to kindly zip it. Research shows forgiving yourself for procrastination is key to boosting productivity and living your best life.

10. Have an accountability partner.

If you're struggling to light a fire under your tasks, think about teaming up with an accountability partner. Finding the right one is crucial. Look for someone who gets why your tasks matter or shares your goals. Could be a family member, a friend, or a colleague who's got your back and isn't afraid to call you out. And make sure their schedule matches yours, because ain't nobody got time for missed check-ins. Lay it all out—how often you'll touch base, how to dish on progress, and what kind of cheerleading you need. Having someone to keep your feet to the fire not only helps you knock out that to-do list but also gives you the push you need to keep pushing forward.

Yep, I know overcoming procrastination isn't a breeze, but hey, you're geared up to get moving. And don't procrastinate on this one, because in the next chapter, we're amping up a crucial mental muscle.

Chapter 3: Enhance Your Focus

Often, I find myself standing in the middle of my kitchen, staring at the refrigerator door like it's going to reveal the secrets of the universe. Why did I come in here? What did I need again? I think for several seconds with no recollection of why I came into the kitchen and leave, only to invariably remember my original purpose an hour later. Sound familiar? Trust me, I know I'm not alone in this. Millions of us lose focus and forget our purpose as we wander through the day, wasting precious time trying to remember what the heck we were doing in the first place.

Research from the University of California San Diego conducted by Adam Aron and Jan Wessel shows that there is a reason for this brain fog; studies of neurons and the system within the brain known as the subthalamic nucleus (STN) show that when we start thinking while we're in action, our brains tend to lose focus if the action gets interrupted or stopped thereby causing us to forget what it is that we intended to do. More often than not, these interruptions are caused by unexpected events, like running into someone as you exit a store[7]

---

[7] Vozza, Stephanie. What Happens In Your Brain When You Lose

Psychologically, the reason for this forgetfulness makes sense; the human body is programmed with an automatic fight-flight-freeze response that kicks in whenever we perceive danger. This hard reset of our memory allows us to use our brain functions to respond to threats and stay safe. Unfortunately, most of the threats we perceive throughout the day are innocuous daily occurrences, the innocent ring of a phone or the sudden appearance of a chatty coworker causing us to frequently forget our purpose and leave us in a perpetual state of befuddlement. Research conducted by David Rock, co-founder of the NeuroLeadership Institute and author of *Your Brain at Work,* has confirmed this; While the average American spends nine hours a day at work, Rock found that we're only productive for about six hours a week due to constant distractions.

Alright, let's cut to the chase. Disruptions are productivity's arch-nemesis, causing us to miss out on valuable opportunities to check off on our to-do lists. Sure, these reactions are hardwired in our brains, thanks to our evolutionary "danger alert" system. But guess what? You can actually train your brain to combat these interruptions, stay focused, and knock out those tasks like a boss, even when life throws you a curveball.

Focus. Fast Company. 2016.
https://www.fastcompany.com/3060388/what-happens-in-your-brain-when-you-lose-focus

How Concentration Works?

Concentration is a top-down process. You've got to consciously put in the effort to zero in on something so you can absorb and analyze all the info thrown your way For example, think about a picture; when you first glance at a photo, your brain takes in the whole image. But the longer you stare, the more you start noticing tiny details and nuances, letting you truly appreciate the piece. When you begin to focus like this, everything else seems to melt away. Outside distractions? Who cares. You're locked in on what's right in front of you.

How Do We Lose Focus?

Okay, here's the twist: losing focus is actually good for you. I know it sounds counterintuitive, but hear me out. Biologically, we're hardwired to zero in on situations that matter most—like when danger's lurking or when there's a reward on the line. Centuries of evolution have shown we need this kind of reaction to survive and thrive. The downside? Try explaining this to your boss when they catch you zoning out in a meeting. Or to your teacher when your mind drifts during a lecture. They're not exactly impressed by your evolutionary prowess.

Losing focus is a productivity killer. Gloria Mark, a professor at the University of California, Irvine, found that once you lose focus it can take up to 25 minutes to return to the task you originally started. A small, one-minute interruption can throw you off for almost half an hour! Now, imagine you're in school or at the office, where distractions pop up every 3-10 minutes. One minute you're deep into drafting that report, and the next, Kristine from accounting is at your desk asking if you've seen the latest office meme or the latest gossip about Sarah from marketing who's apparently dating her yoga instructor. Or you're about to grasp that complex concept in a lecture, and suddenly, your phone buzzes with a notification from that group chat that never sleeps. Maybe you're finally getting into the groove of that spreadsheet when Carl strolls by, wanting to chat about last night's basketball game. Obviously, with all these interruptions, it's no wonder that so little work gets done throughout the week![8]

Many people believe that distractions can dodge distractions at work by avoiding their colleagues, but Mark's research shows that this is not the case. Turns out, we're our own worst enemies—interrupting ourselves 44 percent of the time. So, let's face it: there's no simple, clear-cut way to eliminate distractions from our lives.

---

[8] Mark, Gloria. Gudith, Daniela. Klocke, Ulrich. The Cost of Interrupted Work: More Speed and Stress. 2019.
https://www.ics.uci.edu/~gmark/chi08-mark.pdf

While the research on distraction is damning, there is still a glimmer of hope for our focus game: studies reveal our minds can lock onto a task for a solid two hours. The question remains: how do we reach that holy grail of concentration?

To begin unraveling our full focus potential, let's pinpoint the root cause of our distraction: chronic overwhelm. In today's fast-paced world, we're inundated with an incessant stream of information every minute. Our brains haven't evolved to keep up with this barrage, leaving us feeling disoriented—like squirrels in a hurricane. To cope, we escape into the soothing embrace of distractions—hello, endless scroll of social media feeds and overflowing inbox. Surprise, surprise, this leaves us far less effective at completing necessary tasks.

Distractions aren't just annoying—they're a drain on both our productivity and our sanity. The average office Joe juggles focus like a circus act, switching between ten and twenty times an hour, causing them to lose track of their tasks altogether as they respond to minute-by-minute concerns. This frenetic task-switching isn't just tiresome; it's a mental marathon that leaves us foggy-headed and prone to forgetting where we left our coffee cup, let alone our latest brilliant idea. And as if losing focus wasn't infuriating enough. Research confirms what we've all suspected: every task we triumphantly check off comes at a cost. Our ability to focus diminishes throughout the day, draining our mental resources and making it harder to keep our eyes on the prize. Remember, attention isn't just a luxury; it's a precious, dwindling commodity we can't afford to waste.

Resist Temptation.

Again, distractions are productivity's arch-nemesis—and let's not forget, they're also pretty bad for our sanity. So, how do we dodge these productivity pitfalls? Plan ahead; strategic planning is key to keeping distractions from hijacking your day, as life throws more curveballs than a rookie pitcher.

And when distractions inevitably rear their head, carve out some sacred "distraction-free" zones. Set a specific time to power down your phone and log out of all social media accounts. —basically, anything that could lure you into a vortex of mindless scrolling. Your brain will thank you for the laser-like focus. By disconnecting from these external distractions, you give your brain the freedom to concentrate on the task at hand rather than constantly battling the urge to refresh your Instagram feed every 15 seconds. It's a simple act that can significantly boost your mental performance and keep your productivity levels high throughout the day.

Of course, staying distraction-free isn't a cakewalk. It takes guts and discipline to keep your gaze fixed on the prize. Even the most focused among us can't dodge every shiny object— the brain is wired to pay attention to novelty and anomalies.

Tame Your Internal Distractions.

External distractions – can often be avoided with the click of a button or a strategic hiding spot. But internal distractions? Now that's another beast. They're those lightning-fast, unconscious thoughts that hijack our focus whenever our minds drift. This wandering attention stems from ambient neural activity, or our brain's nervous system constantly processing, reconfiguring, and reconnecting data in your brain non-stop.

Neuroscientists Trey Hedden and John Gabrieli from MIT delved into the impact of internal distractions on individuals tackling challenging tasks. Their findings were clear; people who were consumed by their own thoughts were significantly impaired in their ability to perform the task assigned to them, often without even realizing they were distracted.. This loss of external focus led to decreased productivity.[9]

---

[9] Rock, David. Dr. Beat Back Distractions: The Neuroscience Of Getting Things Done Huffington Post. 2016.
https://www.huffpost.com/entry/beat-back-distractions-

Although it might appear daunting to combat distractions fueled by our own minds, scientific methods offer promising strategies to enhance our focus.

The human brain, inherently designed to maintain focus, can be effectively trained. Neuroscientists employ methods like the Stroop test to assess and improve focus capabilities. In this test, volunteers are given words printed in different colors and instructed to name the color of the text rather than read the word itself aloud. Overcoming the distraction posed by the actual word requires participants to inhibit their automatic responses, enabling them to focus on the task at hand and respond accurately. This scientific approach demonstrates how targeted training can mitigate internal distractions and enhance cognitive performance.

The key to combating internal distractions lies in training the ventrolateral prefrontal cortex (VLPFC), a brain region responsible for inhibition. By enhancing its ability to restrain automatic responses, you can reduce the impact of wandering thoughts and memories that hinder peak performance. When your mind wanders, you become distracted by memories and thoughts, both factual and emotional, which prevent you from being able to work to your full potential. Training your brain to control automatic responses to different stimuli helps block these internal distractions. This proactive approach enhances your focus and productivity, paving the way for greater success in your endeavors.

How do you go about training your brain? It starts with your brain's braking system. In the VLPFC, there is a brake system, much like car, that strongly correlates with how well you can focus. When a car is going down a hill, braking early can allow it time to slow down to make necessary turns and changes to stay on route. Similarly, when we catch a distracting thought early, we can stop ourselves from getting tangled in it and veering off course, redirecting our focus to the task at hand.[10]

Unfortunately, the brake system in our minds is as fragile as it is temperamental. It takes serious energy to resist the brain's urge to wander. Think of it as a form of impulse control – sometimes, you manage to keep yourself in check, focusing on the goal at hand. Other times, those impulses win, and you end up acting on thoughts and desires you know you shouldn't.

To activate your brain's braking system, you need to be aware of your internal mental processes so that you can catch yourself before your thoughts go awry. Timing

---

[10] Rock, David. Easily distracted: why it's hard to focus, and what to do about it. Psychology Today. 2009.
https://www.psychologytoday.com/us/blog/your-brain-work/200910/easily-distracted-why-its-hard-focus-and-what-do-about-it

is everything. Catch a thought early, and you can stop it from becoming a distraction; the earlier you catch the thought, the less energy it takes to rein it back in and refocus g on the task at hand. That's why it's crucial to constantly pay attention to, well, your attention.

The core skill you need to master to fend off internal distractions? Mindfulness.

So, how do you cultivate this magical mindfulness, you ask? Up next, we'll dive into practical strategies to train your brain, harness the power of mindfulness, and finally put an end to those pesky internal distractions. Buckle up, it's time to take control.

Focus Like a Pro

1. The Art of Mindfulness Meditation.

Engaging in regular mindfulness meditation helps you recognize and release thoughts as they come, understanding their transient nature and reducing their power over your focus. When intrusive thoughts arise, acknowledging them and gently redirecting your attention back to your task can enhance your ability to stay productive and handle distractions effectively later on.

Another effective approach to mindfulness is through intentional scheduling. Given our brain's tendency to wander and the inevitable distractions that crop up, it's crucial to structure your day around focused work. By prioritizing complex tasks during your peak concentration times, typically earlier in the day, you maximize productivity and minimize the likelihood of interruptions, setting the stage for accomplishing meaningful work efficiently. For instance, if your job requires creative thinking or deep analysis, schedule these tasks for the morning or the beginning of your workday when your mind is fresh and less cluttered with distractions. This approach allows you to harness your peak mental energy and tackle complex challenges with greater focus and clarity, ensuring you make the most of your productive hours.

Your brain, like any other muscle in your body, needs to be exercised and trained to function at its best. Practicing mindfulness meditation helps you become more aware, giving you the ability to block out distractions and focus for longer periods of time. Research from Emory University underscores this, revealing that dedicating just 20 minutes each day to mindfulness meditation can notably bolster your concentration levels throughout the day.[11]

---

[11] Hasenkamp, W., & Barsalou, L. W. (2012). Effects of meditation experience on functional connectivity of distributed brain networks. Frontiers in human neuroscience, 6, 38. doi:10.3389/fnhum.2012.00038

Mindfulness meditation can be as straightforward as closing your eyes, taking deep breaths, and directing your attention to a chosen focal point. If you're new to meditation, it's a simple practice that can seamlessly integrate into your daily routine. Numerous meditation programs and podcasts are available to assist you in achieving a mindful, relaxed state. You can check out online guided meditation apps such as Calm or Headspace. Alternatively, joining a meditation group can provide effective guidance and support to cultivate your mindfulness practice consistently.

2. Shut the Door.

Whenever interruptions disrupt our tasks, it can take 27% longer to complete even the simplest to-dos. Additionally, distractions increase the likelihood of errors and heighten anxiety over task completion. To mitigate this, it's crucial to establish physical boundaries that separate us from distractions in our workspace.

If possible, close your workspace door to keep out any unwanted distractions and signal your coworkers that you are focused on work. When a door isn't an option, consider an alternative "door" that you can use to shut people out, like a pair of quality headphones. Having your headphones on can also signal your coworkers that you are unavailable at the moment and can provide you with some noise to block out any potentially distracting sounds in your environment, thus enhancing concentration on your tasks.

3. The Power of Short Breaks.

Breaks are important for productivity. Research shows that the human brain's optimal focus span is about two hours. Beyond this, performance declines rapidly. To maximize productivity, experts suggest taking short breaks every 40 minutes. This limitation occurs because our short-term memory can only handle a limited amount of information—typically between 5 to 9 items at a time. Exceeding this capacity overwhelms our brains, leading to decreased efficiency and cognitive shutdown.

Taking breaks is crucial for maintaining productivity, even though many believe continuous work leads to greater output. I kid you not, incorporating breaks into your routine is a vital factor in enhancing both personal and professional productivity. Life is full of moments of pause – we pause between breaths, between songs, and even when we speak – and these moments of pause should also extend to our work sessions. When we skip breaks, we quickly lose focus and our cognitive resources dwindle, leading to reduced productivity over time—a phenomenon known as vigilance decrement in psychology. Science continues to show that the brain needs breaks to save data and refresh its capacity to continue processing new information.

However, integrating breaks into our work routine isn't as straightforward as it seems, we often are unable to draw the boundary between taking a break and procrastinating. To avoid the procrastination pitfall in taking a break, consider scheduling breaks using the Pomodoro Technique varying break frequencies and durations. Scheduled short breaks (10-20 minutes) enable focused work sessions, enhancing productivity and allowing for longer periods of intense concentration. These breaks should serve a purpose, rejuvenating your mind with activities such as catching up with loved ones, enjoying a coffee break, or taking a stroll.

To use breaks effectively, we must overcome the stigma that taking them is shameful. Many feel guilty, fearing it makes them appear lazy or unproductive, questioning, "What would my father think if he saw me taking a break right now when I should be working?" By understanding why we feel this guilt, we can address it objectively, recognizing breaks as essential for regaining energy and focus, ultimately enhancing long-term productivity over short-term task completion and reducing guilt about taking necessary breaks.

4. The Pomodoro Technique.

The Pomodoro Technique is a brain-training program designed to enhance your ability to concentrate and stay focused on tasks for longer periods of time. Using the Pomodoro Technique, you train your brain using the same type of interval training you would use for other muscles of your body; you set a timer for 25 minutes to intensely focus, followed by a 5-minute break to handle any distractions After every four 25-minute periods, you allow yourself to take a longer break (20-30 minutes in length) to recoup your strength. This method builds your endurance gradually, allowing you to tackle larger projects more effectively. If 25 minutes seems daunting, start with shorter intervals like 10-15 minutes and work your way up—it's all about training your focus muscle!

5. Ditch Multitasking.

Think you're a multitasking wizard? Science says otherwise. Turns out, juggling tasks doesn't boost productivity—it tanks by 20-40%! Studies show that multitasking decreases our ability to concentrate by 20-40 percent because our short-term memories can only store between five to nine things at once, making it difficult to balance two separate sets of information to retain and act on them. Instead of enhancing efficiency, multitasking often leaves us spreading ourselves thin, distracted, and unable to fully focus on any one thing. It's a habit fueled by a culture that celebrates busyness and glorifies workaholism, but ditching multitasking could be the key to reclaiming your focus and productivity.

6. Remember Your Whys.

Successful people understand that the key to productivity lies not just in knowing what needs to be done, but in deeply understanding why each task matters. Whether it's a small task or a major project, connecting it to your goals and motivations provides a powerful boost. By reminding yourself of the purpose behind each task—how it contributes to your larger goals or why it matters—you cultivate a positive mindset and clearer focus. This intrinsic motivation not only makes concentrating easier but also drives you to complete tasks efficiently and with purpose.

7. Declutter Your Domain

Your environment plays a crucial role in your ability to concentrate and tackle tasks effectively. A well-organized workspace not only cuts down on distractions but also primes your mindset for productivity. Knowing where everything is and having easy access to your materials minimizes time wasted searching and maximizes your readiness to dive into your work. When your environment supports your goals, you naturally feel more motivated and positive about getting things done.

Want to supercharge your focus through organization? I will dedicate an entire chapter to answer this question later in this book but for now here is a hors d'oeuvre: start by clearing away anything that is not work-related from your designated work area. This simple step reduces visual and physical clutter, creating a distraction-free zone where you can focus exclusively on your daily priorities.

Additionally, many people find that an organized file system is a lifesaver. It ensures they know exactly where all their documents are, saving them precious time from rummaging through bags, files, and folders. And remember, tuck your cell phone away on silent, out of sight. This small act keeps you from constant distractions and lets you stay fully immersed in your tasks.

Chapter 4: Boost Your Productivity

The whole point of having a to-do list is to get more stuff done, right? I mean, most of us turn those lists into these epic sagas that just take over our lives. Then, instead of being super productive, we end up running around like headless chickens. Remember the last time your list was crammed with too much stuff—you probably spent the whole day frantically checking things off. But here's what you *really* did: you spent just as much time dealing with the chaos from dropping the ball here and there. So instead of being a productivity god, you ended up less productive, thanks to your over-ambitious list.

Instead of stressing over a million tasks, why not boost your productivity by focusing on a few key things each day? Prioritize what's really important, get those done thoroughly, and avoid the whole mess of having to fix stuff later because you half-assed it the first time. Trust me, it will do wonders.

It's super important to have a plan for your day so you can create a set schedule for when things need to get done. Even a loose schedule helps you map out your day around your to-do list and set mini-goals. Think about those crazy days at the office: without a plan, it's easy to feel swamped by the endless tasks piling up. But if you set specific times for your tasks, you'll have a more productive and satisfying day, knowing you've got both work and breaks scheduled. And of course, if something takes less time than expected, just tweak your schedule. That way, you can fit more into your day without everything going off the rails.

Another thing that might be messing with your productivity? Your emotional, physical, or mental state. Seriously, how you feel can totally make or break your day.

Let me tell you about my colleague Leticia. She woke up with a nasty toothache but decided to head to work because, you know, bills don't pay themselves. She tried to eat breakfast, but the pain was too much.

That discomfort started gnawing at her mood, making her uneasy. And with that mental state, she snapped at our boss—who, bless his heart, was just asking for a project update. Thankfully, our understanding boss advised her to take some time off when he learned about her toothache, but the project had to be delayed.

If Leticia had addressed her toothache immediately, things might have gone smoother. My point is when physical pain, emotional strain, and mental stress pile up, no one is spared.

You see, our brains just aren't wired to juggle emotions and work at the same time. Stress and pain crank up the production of hormones like cortisol, which can really mess with our decision-making skills if we don't handle them. So, when you're trying to focus on a task but feel stressed out, it's no surprise you struggle to get things done.

How do you beat this productivity killer? By making your physical, emotional and mental well-being a priority, you set yourself up for long-term success. In simpler terms, take care of yourself first. If you don't know where to start, you can always visit a doctor for advice. When you're well-maintained and firing on all cylinders, the chances of breakdowns decrease significantly.

If the previous advice sounds overwhelming, here's some good news for you. Another thing to boost productivity is to literally do nothing. Do nothing as in meditate. There's this technique called "Noting Practice". It goes like this: whenever some pesky thought or feeling

---

[12] Neff, K. (2015). Self-Compassion: The Proven Power of Being Kind to Yourself. HarperCollins.

barges into your mind, just give it a soft mental note. Like, "Oh hey, there's anger again," or "Hmm, anxiety making a cameo." This little trick makes you more aware of what's going on inside your head. Once you clock that emotion as a passing blip instead of a lifelong condition, you're back in the driver's seat. You see you can choose how to handle this fleeting feeling. It doesn't own you—these brief thoughts won't steer your ship. Now, you can shift gears and do your next move with clarity and purpose.

To maintain peak productivity, it's crucial to stay mindful of daily habits that might impede your ability to focus fully. Here are some tips to enhance productivity and ensure you're checking off your to-do list:

Productivity Tips

1. Cut down on the constant email checking.

Research reveals a staggering number of us check email incessantly—22% up to ten times daily and 9% over 40 times! Julie Morgenstern, Oprah's guru, warns in *Never Check Email in the Morning* that this habit kills productivity by tackling immediate tasks while important ones linger. To break free, schedule specific times each day for email—just **two** periods max—and set strict limits to avoid getting sucked in. Turn off notifications on all devices to focus on urgent tasks without interruptions. If the thought of limiting email checks scares you, dig into why—it could be boredom or fear of missing out. Address these triggers head-on for a more focused, less disrupted workday.

2. Practice self-care.

Look, I get it—self-care can feel like the last thing you have time for when your to-do list is a mile long. But here's why it's important: prioritizing yourself is actually key to getting stuff done. When you neglect your physical and mental well-being, it catches up with you, big time. Remember that rushed desk lunch or quick fast-food fix during a crazy workday? Yeah, not exactly fuel for greatness. Taking care of yourself isn't just a luxury—it's a necessity for staying sharp and productive. So, make time for those real meals, hit the reset button with a walk or meditation break, and watch how it boosts your game. You owe it to yourself, and your to-do list will thank you for it later.

Bad health habits don't just mess with your waistline; they mess with your work game, too. Scarfing down candy or chugging cola might give you a quick jolt, but that crash is coming—hard. Your brain needs the good stuff—nutritious food and solid sleep—to stay on point. Skimping on either is like running on empty. Whenever you're tempted to skip meals or burn the midnight oil, think about the toll it takes on your productivity. Treat your body right, and watch how much sharper you'll feel all day long. You've got goals to crush—fuel up and get after them!

To master self-care, prioritize your DSE—diet, sleep, and exercise—they're your secret weapons for top health, clear thinking, and crushing every day.

A. Diet

Make a weekly plan for stocking up on wholesome foods and prepping ahead. Having these ready saves you from those tempting junk food pitfalls at work. Keep a list of no-gos (like chips and cookies) nearby as a visual reminder to stay on track when healthier options aren't in reach. Plan your meals in advance to sidestep impulsive choices and stick to a consistent eating schedule. This approach keeps you energized and focused, ready to conquer every hour of your day.

B. Sleep

Avoid burning the midnight oil by setting a bedtime alarm 30 minutes before lights out. Use this time to unwind and set the stage for a restful night like a pro. With a solid 7-hour recharge, you'll wake up feeling refreshed and unstoppable, ready to tackle whatever comes your way with clarity and vigor.

C. Exercise

Commit to at least 30 minutes a day—whether it's biking, jogging, dancing, or yoga. Regular cardiovascular activity three times a week boosts brain power, sharpens focus, and amps up those feel-good vibes. Find an exercise you love and fits your lifestyle, no need for fancy gyms or big commitments. Embrace movement as a vital part of your day to elevate your health and productivity goals. You've got this!

3. Master the art of saying "no."

Sure, being the go-to helper for everyone from your nosy neighbor to your office mates might score you some popularity points, but it won't do squat for your productivity. Taking on tasks that aren't even your responsibility adds to your already overflowing to-do list without even checking if it aligns with your own priorities. Remember that time you volunteered to save the day at the office? I know it felt good and earned you that "helpful" gold star, but now you've set a precedent. Suddenly, everyone expects you to be their superhero, leaving your own work in the dust. And guess what? People catch on quickly. Soon enough, your kindness becomes an open invitation for others to pile on more, leaving you feeling drained and behind on what actually matters.

Setting boundaries with your willingness to help—like offering partial assistance or politely explaining you're busy but available later—lets you prioritize your own tasks while keeping relationships positive.

4. Stop being a control freak.

Ever heard of The Beatles' hit song "With a Little Help from My Friends"? (If you don't, listen to it now!) It's the perfect personal productivity anthem.

While letting go of control can be tough, one of the best ways to boost productivity is by working together and assigning tasks to those nearby. Have you ever had to handle a long list of tasks in one day? I have, and let me tell you—the feeling sucks. It left me frustrated, overwhelmed, and unable to finish everything.

Before you even raise your brows and tell me that delegation makes someone look weak, let's debunk this myth: handing off tasks doesn't make you look like a slacker. In fact, those who can juggle, prioritize, and delegate as needed come off as more on top of things than those drowning in their to-do lists. And if you're clinging to control because you want everything done perfectly, consider whether you've got the bandwidth for that. Delegating often means you can focus intensely on fewer tasks, nailing each one with precision. And when you hesitate to ask for backup, just ask yourself, "What's the worst that could happen?" Usually, the benefits of sharing the load far outweigh any downside you're imagining.

If you're scared to delegate, try prioritizing your to-do list. Split it up into short-term and long-term tasks, then focus on the 3-5 tasks that really need your touch of genius. Look through the rest and spot the ones that are easily fixable or won't tank the universe if they're not perfect. This way, you'll see which tasks are worth keeping on your plate and which ones you can happily pass off to someone else to lighten your load and boost your own game.

In the end, it's all about valuing your time. Take a good look at your to-do list and seriously ask yourself: is sacrificing time with your squad worth ticking off those chores? Your time is pure gold, and once you really understand that, you can start making choices that align with what truly matters—whether it's kicking back with loved ones or getting stuff done. Getting this mindset down is key to loosening your grip a bit and letting others step in where they can help. And if you're not sure who's got your back, start by listing your go-to hustlers. Having this crew ready to roll will make delegating a breeze.

5. Create a system for recurring tasks.

One of the most common time-wasting habits is duplicating efforts on recurring tasks, which can significantly diminish productivity. Whether it's a daily, weekly, monthly, or yearly task, implementing a systematic approach ensures consistency and efficiency, optimizing your workflow and guaranteeing task completion with precision.

To combat this productivity drain, begin by cataloging all recurring tasks and assessing the time spent on each. Develop tailored systems to streamline these tasks. For instance, if you regularly send promotional emails every Monday, allocate an hour on the first Monday of each month to draft and schedule these emails in advance. This proactive approach frees up your time and mental energy for more critical activities.

When setting up systems for recurring tasks like this, be sure to schedule them on your calendar or use an app like Tweek, Trello, or Todoist. This ensures you stay organized and remember to tackle all your tasks efficiently in one go. By doing so, you'll minimize ongoing work and maximize productivity throughout the month.

6. Own up to your actions.

Dodging responsibility is like putting handcuffs on your potential to thrive in your work. When you view tasks as burdens, it's easy to fall into procrastination and settle for less than your best, which holds you back from seizing career opportunities and growth. Your mindset is everything—owning your actions starts with understanding how it shapes your outcomes. Take a fearless look at why you shy away from responsibility and where that habit stems from. Owning up isn't just about claiming victories but also learning from missteps to propel yourself forward. It might feel easier to pass the blame when things go sideways, but taking ownership is where personal and professional growth truly begins. Be your own biggest advocate on this journey, showing up with kindness and determination to break through barriers and achieve your goals.

7. Quit wallowing in self-pity.

We all get it—life can really suck sometimes. But let me tell you something straight: sitting around in your self-pity party is useless. Complaining and feeling sorry for yourself? That's just a one-way ticket to draining your mojo and staying stuck in that same old rut. Sure, venting might give you a momentary high, but it's not gonna magically help you get back on track or tackle those challenges staring you down.

Instead of dwelling on what's going wrong, take a good, hard look at your role in the situation. Maybe you've been shouldering too much because others aren't pulling their weight, or you've let negativity overshadow your potential solutions. Recognizing these patterns is your ticket to reclaiming control over your life. Once you've gained that clarity, shift gears towards proactive solutions and actionable steps. This mindset not only empowers you to make positive changes but also channels your energy into things that propel you forward.

8. Pregame your meetings.

To boost your productivity, always research and prepare for your meetings. Before stepping into any meeting, remind yourself of its purpose and the outcomes you aim to achieve. If discussions veer off-topic, gently steer them back to focus on the meeting's goals. This approach ensures you achieve desired results efficiently.

Step out of your own head and share those ideas. When you brainstorm and collaborate with your coworkers, it's like adding some extra spice to your favorite dish – it just gets better.

By mixing everyone's perspectives, you boost your productivity and effectiveness. Your original idea gets a nice little upgrade, and you save yourself a ton of time and energy down the road. Trust me, don't be shy – put your thoughts out there and let the magic happen!

But, wait, just one more thing: just reading about productivity won't turn you into a productivity wizard. It's the *doing* that comes after the reading. Pick a few solid tips, turn them into habits, and then take massive action. That's the secret sauce. So, what are you waiting for.   Just.   Freaking.   Do.   It!

Chapter 5: How to Become More Organized

Getting organized isn't just a nice-to-have—it's the secret sauce to powering through your to-do list and ramping up your productivity. Despite what you might think, being organized isn't a genetic gift; it's a skill honed through practice and habit. People with great organizational skills are not born this way; rather, they have spent years cultivating healthy habits to stay organized and approach their work efficiently. Even if you're the poster child for chaos, you can learn to stay organized with small, simple changes to your daily routine. Skeptical? Try these suggestions to kickstart positive changes and become more organized.

1. Unlock Your Memory with Simple Notes.

Are you struggling to remember dates and deadlines in your head? Try writing them down! Research indicates that jotting down important information increases the likelihood of remembering it later. This technique not only reinforces the information in your memory but also gives you a tangible reminder of tasks, like remembering to send a birthday card! When in doubt, write it out!

To make this habit easier, carry a notebook for your thoughts. Write your grocery lists, important dates, to-do lists, and other important information here to help jog your memory later down the line! Trust me, your future self will thank you!

2. **Everything in Its Place.**

The best way to stay organized is to give everything in your life a home. When you have a specific place for everything, you keep order in your physical space, reducing the distractions and clutter in your brain.

Start your organization with the things you use every day, and give them homes that are easy for you to access. If, for example, you frequently have to staple documents together, ensure your stapler has a home near your workspace, so you don't have to constantly get up to use it. A label maker can be a game-changer here, helping you define spaces for each item and maintain that sweet, sweet order.

Make sure everything is intentionally placed and labeled; the biggest pitfall people fall prey to when organizing is creating a "miscellaneous" drawer. This can quickly become a clutter magnet, so avoid throwing together miscellaneous items at all costs. And for an extra boost of inspiration, check out Marie Kondo's work. Her bestselling book *The Life Changing Magic of Tidying Up* and Netflix series offer fantastic tips on how to declutter and organize everything efficiently and beautifully. Embrace these methods, and watch your space and productivity transform.

3. Cleaning Out the Wardrobe: Tidy, Keep, Declutter.

Managing tasks is akin to maintaining a well-organized wardrobe—tidy up, prioritize what's essential, and declutter the rest to enhance productivity.

Tidy Up: Life is messy, and your environment won't stay organized on its own. Constant and consistent reorganization is key to preventing your space from becoming chaotic. Dedicate your time and energy to the most important tasks on your to-do list, and remove anything that's not essential.

Keep What's Essential: Just as you keep essential wardrobe items within reach, prioritize tasks that align with your objectives. Take a cue from organized coworkers: they maintain a clutter-free space by keeping only what's necessary, which allows them to fully utilize and enjoy their belongings.

Not sure if you have too much stuff? Take out a piece of paper and jot down everything you use throughout the day in each room. Once your list is complete, evaluate everything else in the room that seems unnecessary. Often, you'll find items that could be cleared out to simplify your life and create a more organized environment. Wanna know more on decluttering? Your wish is my command, coming up next!

Declutter: Take a tour of your living and working spaces and identify tools that haven't seen use in months or even years. Do you really need these objects? Ditch the "it may come in handy one day" mindset. For instance, if you've amassed a collection of empty margarine jars under the guise of future hair dye projects, consider keeping just one for practicality and parting with the rest.

Once you've decided to part with items, know where they can go. Methodically go through each room, creating three piles—keep, toss, and donate/sell. After sorting through your belongings, follow through: items you're keeping should find their designated spots, while those destined for disposal should head to the donation drive, recycling center or trash. Donate or sell unwanted items through thrift stores, eBay, Craigslist, or local flea markets. This approach not only clears unnecessary clutter but also focuses your efforts on maintaining what truly matters in your space.

4. Delegating Chores or Sharing Tasks

Delegation is a key strategy they employ to reduce stress and enhance their organizational skills. Just as managing household tasks requires guidance and teamwork, so does tackling your to-do list effectively. Those with strong organizational skills understand the value of delegation—they enlist help from friends, family, and colleagues to lighten their workload and ensure everything gets done efficiently.

Unconvinced on how task delegation can help you get more organized? Go through your to-do list and find just one task that you can ask another person to do, and let it go. Getting help on tasks can alleviate stress and make you feel more in control of your workload.

Conclusion

You see, organizing isn't just a task—it's a rare masterpiece skill. Each step in this organizational process is crucial for maximizing productivity and achieving tangible progress toward your goals. Crafting a to-do list isn't just about jotting down tasks; it's about mapping out a strategic plan for your day, week, month, or even year. Again, as repetitive as I might sound, this will help you sharpen your focus, keep you on track, and significantly boost your productivity.

When you become more effective in all these areas, your overall organizational skills will improve. You'll better understand why you're completing each task and how you're going to complete them. Don't you worry, this clarity means you'll no longer be distracted by everyday life. Instead, you'll get more done in less time.

If you take anything away from this book, let it be this: organization is a journey, not a destination. Each of us is on our own organizational journey, learning new skills to realize our full potential and achieve our goals. It is my hope that this book has inspired you to take charge of your life and adopt new habits that will boost your productivity and allow you to live a more organized, less cluttered life.

Thank you, hon, for taking this journey with me; your commitment to bettering your life is truly commendable, and you are already better for having taken this proactive step toward a more organized future. As you continue your journey, remember how far you've come. Be proud of your progress—you've made it this far, and you can go the distance. One dog at the time.

    Best of luck,
    Michelle

Did you like this book?

I'd really appreciate it if you could leave a review on Amazon – whether you love it or hate it, any feedback is welcome – it'll either make me swoon or teach me a thing or two.

Thanks a lot for coming along on this journey. I hope something from this sticks with you and changes your life.

Reference

Allen, David. Getting Things Done. Downloaded in 2019. www.davidco.com

Babauta, Leo. Purpose Your Day: Most Important Task (MIT). Zen Habits. 2019. https://zenhabits.net/purpose-your-day-most-important-task/

Hasenkamp, W., & Barsalou, L. W. (2012). Effects of meditation experience on functional connectivity of distributed brain networks. Frontiers in human neuroscience, 6, 38. doi:10.3389/fnhum.2012.00038

Knapp, J., & Zeratsky, J. (2018). Make time: How to focus on what matters every day. Currency.

Mark, Gloria. Gudith, Daniela. Klocke, Ulrich. The Cost of Interrupted Work: More Speed and Stress. 2019. https://www.ics.uci.edu/~gmark/chi08-mark.pdf

Milliken, K., & Pickard, M. (2016). PlayDHD: Permission to play ... a prescription for adults with ADHD. Kirsten Milliken.

Neff, K. (2015). Self-Compassion: The Proven Power of Being Kind to Yourself. HarperCollins.

Robbins, Mel. The Five-Second Rule. Savio Republic. 2017.

Rock, David. Dr. Beat Back Distractions: The Neuroscience Of Getting Things Done Huffington Post. 2016. https://www.huffpost.com/entry/beat-back-distractions-th_n_498120

Rock, David. Easily distracted: why it's hard to focus, and what to do about it. Psychology Today. 2009. https://www.psychologytoday.com/us/blog/your-brain-work/200910/easily-distracted-why-its-hard-focus-and-what-do-about-it

Sinek, S. (2017). Find your why: A practical guide for discovering purpose for you and your team. Penguin Random House.

Vozza, Stephanie. What Happens In Your Brain When You Lose Focus. Fast Company. 2016. https://www.fastcompany.com/3060388/what-happens-in-your-brain-when-you-lose-focus

Vrabie, Alina. The science behind concentration and improved focus. Sandglaz. 2013.

https://blog.sandglaz.com/the-science-behind-concentration/

Endnotes

---

[1] Babauta, Leo. Purpose Your Day: Most Important Task (MIT). Zen Habits. 2019. https://zenhabits.net/purpose-your-day-most-important-task/

[2] Allen, David. Getting Things Done. Downloaded in 2019. www.davidco.com

[3] Robbins, Mel. The Five-Second Rule. Savio Republic. 2017.

[4] Sinek, S. (2017). Find your why: A practical guide for discovering purpose for you and your team. Penguin Random House.

[5] Knapp, J., & Zeratsky, J. (2018). Make time: How to focus on what matters every day. Currency.

[6] Milliken, K., & Pickard, M. (2016). PlayDHD: Permission to play ... a prescription for adults with ADHD. Kirsten Milliken.

[7] Vozza, Stephanie. What Happens In Your Brain When You Lose Focus. Fast Company. 2016. https://www.fastcompany.com/3060388/what-happens-in-your-brain-when-you-lose-focus

[8] Mark, Gloria. Gudith, Daniela. Klocke, Ulrich. The Cost of Interrupted Work: More Speed and Stress. 2019. https://www.ics.uci.edu/~gmark/chi08-mark.pdf

[9] Rock, David. Dr. Beat Back Distractions: The Neuroscience Of Getting Things Done Huffington Post. 2016. https://www.huffpost.com/entry/beat-back-distractions-th_n_498120

[10] Rock, David. Easily distracted: why it's hard to focus, and what to do about it. Psychology Today. 2009. https://www.psychologytoday.com/us/blog/your-brain-work/200910/easily-distracted-why-its-hard-focus-and-what-do-about-it

[11] Hasenkamp, W., & Barsalou, L. W. (2012). Effects of meditation experience on functional connectivity of distributed brain networks. Frontiers in human neuroscience, 6, 38.
doi:10.3389/fnhum.2012.00038

[12] Neff, K. (2015). Self-Compassion: The Proven Power of Being Kind to Yourself. HarperCollins.

Made in United States
Troutdale, OR
09/19/2024